SPECTRUM
READERS

S0-ADY-074

BLAST!
Into Space

By Lisa Kurkov

Carson-Dellosa
Publishing

SPECTRUM®

An imprint of Carson-Dellosa Publishing, LLC
P.O. Box 35665
Greensboro, NC 27425-5665

carsondellosa.com

Printed in the USA. All rights reserved.
ISBN 978-1-4838-0126-1

01-002141120

Humans are fascinated by space.
Early humans wondered about the stars
and the moon.
Through modern technology, astronauts
and scientists have begun to explore what
lies beyond our planet.
Little by little, humans are putting
together the puzzles of
the universe.

Satellites

An object that orbits a planet is called a *satellite*.

The moon is Earth's only natural satellite. In 1957, the Soviet Union launched *Sputnik*, the first human-made satellite. *Sputnik* was only the size of a beach ball. It kicked off a space race between countries and led to the founding of NASA—the National Aeronautics and Space Administration.

Fun Facts

- Fruit flies were the first living things to travel into space and safely return.
- Today, satellites transmit phone calls, TV shows, weather reports, maps, and more.

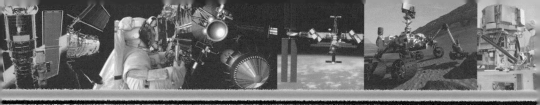

Gemini

The *Gemini* space capsule helped pave the way to the moon.
It flew two unmanned flights in 1964.
In 1965, it carried astronauts into space.
Gemini was small.
It held only two passengers.
The capsule's flight could last two weeks.
The astronauts practiced skills they would need on missions to the moon one day.

Fun Facts

- *Gemini* was so small that astronauts could not stand up inside!

- *Gemini* weighed 8,000 pounds—about the weight of a baby blue whale.

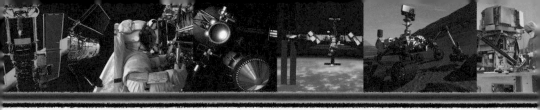

Moon Voyage

In July of 1969, NASA launched *Apollo 11*.
The spacecraft carried Buzz Aldrin, Neil
Armstrong, and Michael Collins.
They took off from the Kennedy Space
Center in Florida.
Earth grew smaller beneath them as they
rose higher and higher.
Apollo 11 reached the moon in three and
a half days.

Fun Facts

- Before their trip, *Apollo* astronauts visited a volcano with craters similar to the moon's surface.

- Only 12 people have walked on the moon. All were American men.

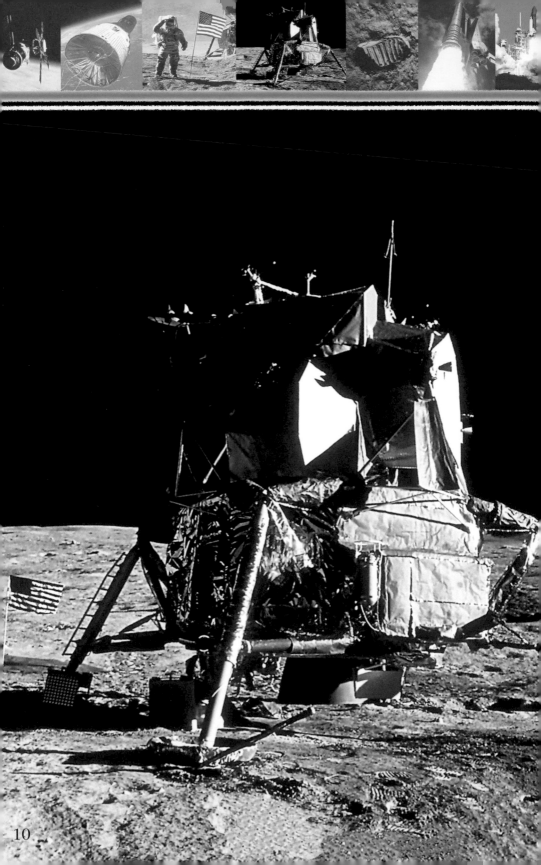

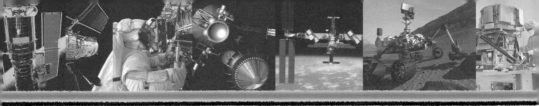

Lunar Module

Apollo 11 astronauts Aldrin and Armstrong boarded a lunar module. It carried them from *Apollo* to the surface of the moon. As soon as they touched down, they practiced lifting off. They wanted to be able to leave quickly! The lunar module carried cameras. They allowed people on Earth to watch the astronauts on TV.

Fun Facts

- The lunar module could operate only in space. It could not fly in Earth's atmosphere.
- A lunar module helped astronauts survive when there was an accident on *Apollo 13*.

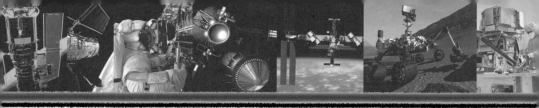

Moon Walk

On July 20, 1969, Neil Armstrong became the first human to walk on the moon.

He spoke the famous words, "That's one small step for [a] man, one giant leap for mankind."

Next, Armstrong and Aldrin found samples of rocks to bring home.

They also planted an American flag in the ground.

That flag still stands on the moon today.

Fun Facts

- A lunar roving vehicle (or moon buggy) helped astronauts get around.

- Armstrong and Aldrin spent **21 hours** on the moon.

First Shuttle

A space shuttle is part spaceship, part rocket, and part airplane.

NASA's shuttle program started in 1981 with the creation of *Columbia*.

Unlike earlier spacecraft, space shuttles were reusable and could be used to launch and repair satellites.

They were also used to build the International Space Station.

Fun Facts

- A space shuttle takes only 90 minutes to travel around the world.
- To escape gravity, a rocket has to travel more than seven miles per second.

Shuttle Program

After *Columbia*, four other shuttles traveled into space: *Challenger*, *Discovery*, *Atlantis*, and *Endeavour*.
They flew a total of 135 missions.
In 2011, the space shuttle program ended.
Two shuttles, *Columbia* and *Challenger*, were lost in accidents.
The others are displayed in museums.

Fun Facts

- Sally Ride was the first American woman in space. She rode *Challenger* in 1983.

- NASA is working on new spacecraft to send humans deeper into space.

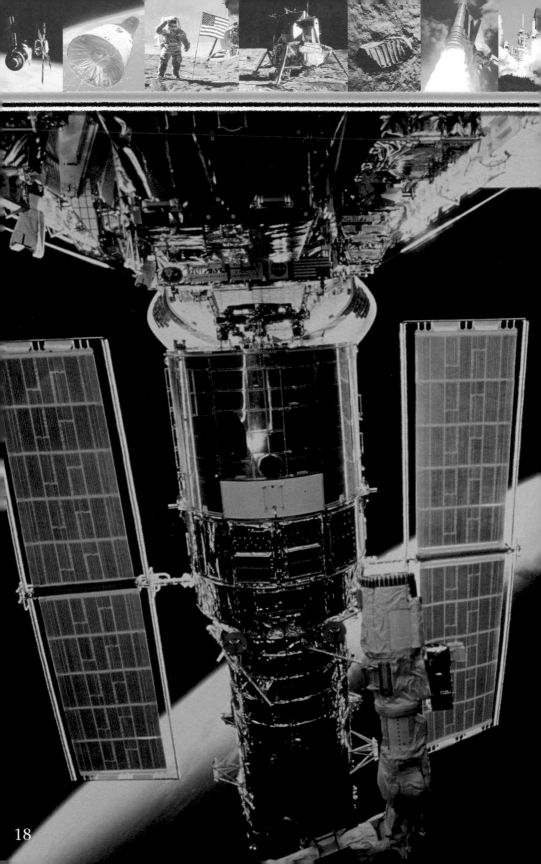

Launching Hubble

In 1990, the shuttle *Discovery* launched the Hubble Space Telescope.

The Hubble is the size of a school bus.

It orbits about 370 miles above Earth.

NASA scientists on the ground control it.

They tell the Hubble where to point.

Then, the huge telescope takes pictures and records data.

Fun Facts

- In 2008, the Hubble took a picture of a planet outside our solar system orbiting another sun!

- In 2018, a new telescope will replace the Hubble.

Space Pictures

The Hubble photographs things we have no other way of seeing, like the births and deaths of stars.

Thanks to the Hubble, we can see black holes and other galaxies.

When a comet crashed into Jupiter in 1994, the Hubble sent images back to Earth.

Fun Facts

- The Hubble was almost a failure. It had a problem with one of its mirrors. Luckily, a shuttle mission fixed it!

- The Hubble orbits Earth once every 97 minutes.

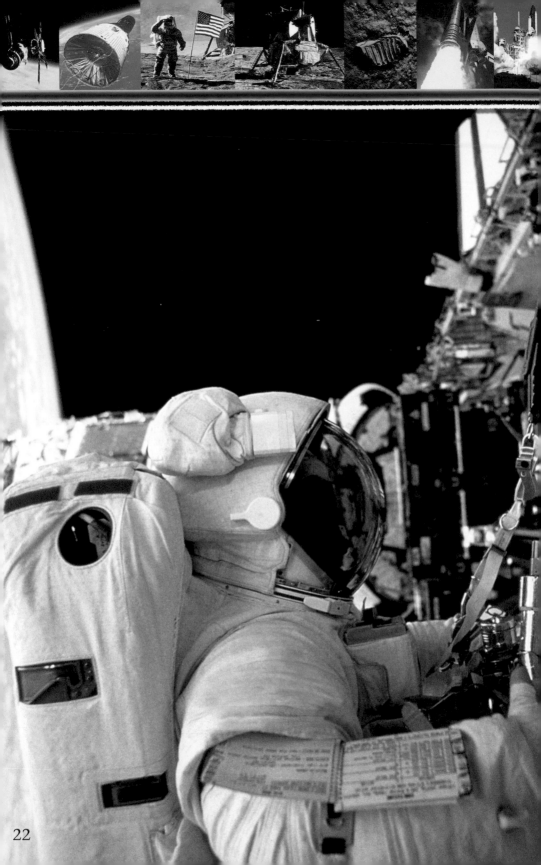

Hubble Repairs

The Hubble Telescope has needed repairs.
The astronauts who fixed it trained
underwater.
This gave them an idea of what it would be
like to work in space.
They traveled on a space shuttle.
They connected the shuttle to the telescope.
Then, they made repairs and updates.

Fun Facts

- Solar panels create all the energy the Hubble needs.
- So far, astronauts have made five repair trips to the Hubble.

Space Probes

Space probes are sent to explore space.
They send information back to Earth.
Probes have reached all the planets in our solar system.
Galileo (pictured) studied Jupiter.
It sent scientists data about Jupiter's atmosphere.
Then, it melted in Jupiter's extreme heat.

Fun Facts

- The probe *BepiColombo* will be launched in 2015. It will reach Mercury in 2022!

- The probe *Voyager 2* made a "grand tour" of Jupiter, Saturn, Uranus, and Neptune.

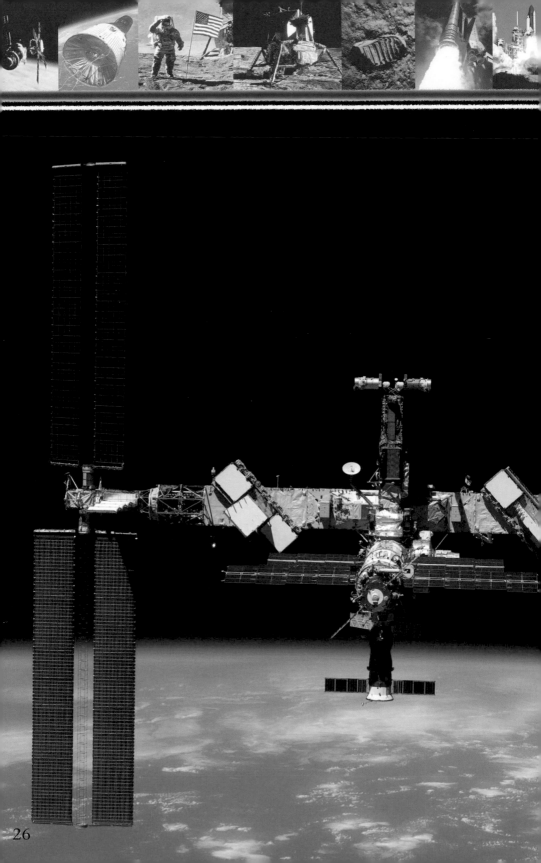

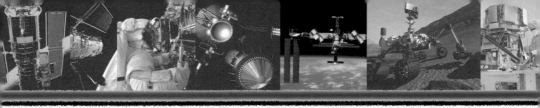

Space Station

In 1998, the International Space Station (ISS) was created by many countries working together.
The ISS was too big to launch at once, so it was built in pieces.
It orbits Earth every 90 minutes.
Up to seven astronauts can live on the station for a few months at a time.

Fun Facts

- Since the ISS travels so fast, astronauts see the sun rise and set 16 times a day!
- The ISS is about the size of a football field. It weighs more than 300 cars!

Exploring Mars

People have always been curious about the planet Mars.

It resembles Earth more than any other planet in our solar system.

In 1997, the rover *Sojourner* took pictures and gathered rocks on Mars.

Rovers *Spirit* and *Opportunity* found evidence of water there in 2004.

In 2012, the *Curiosity* rover began searching Mars for water and other compounds important for life.

Fun Facts

- In 2008, a spacecraft called a *lander* found ice on Mars.

- In the 2030s, astronauts hope to travel to Mars for the first time!

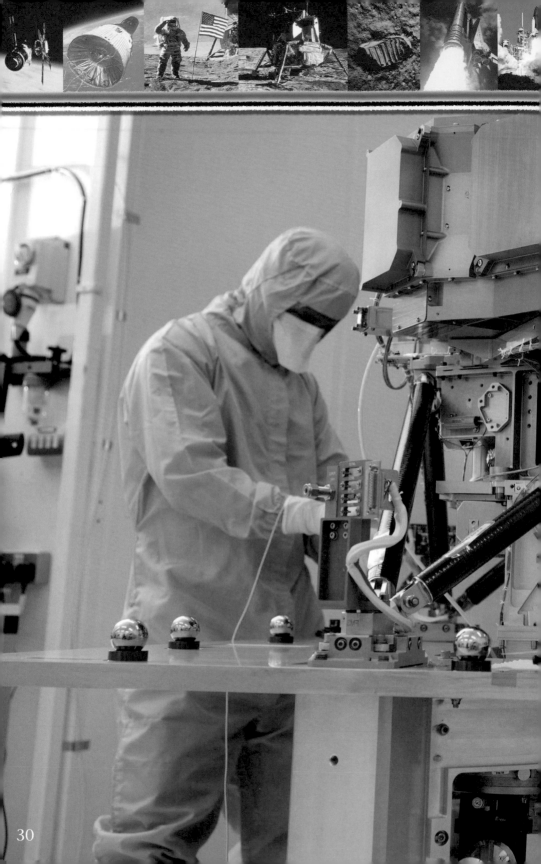

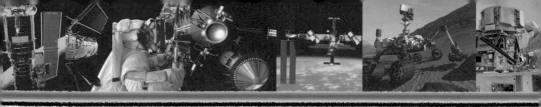

The Future

What is the future of space exploration?
Technology is advancing every day.
Scientists may set up a base on the moon.
Humans might build a colony on Mars.
Think of all we have learned about the
universe in the last few decades.
What mysteries will be unlocked in your
lifetime?

Fun Facts

- Astronauts hope to travel to near-Earth asteroids. Minerals and other resources might be found there.

- One day, the moon or the ISS might be used as a base for launches into space.

BLAST! Into Space
Comprehension Questions

1. What is a satellite?

2. What was the mission of *Apollo 11*?

3. What famous words did Neil Armstrong say as he walked on the moon?

4. How were space shuttles different from earlier spacecraft?

5. Name three shuttles that were part of NASA's shuttle program.

6. What is the Hubble, and why is it important?

7. Name one thing the Hubble has photographed.

8. Which planet in our solar system is most similar to Earth?

9. What exciting discovery did rovers *Spirit* and *Opportunity* make on Mars?

10. Which probe studied the planet Jupiter?